LIVING With

MY LIVED EXPERIENCE

IT'S TIME FOR A CHANGE!

By Dr. Anthony T. Craft

Living with PTSD – My Personal Experience

ISBN: 9798485462086

Published by:
Kindle Direct Publishing

Living with PTSD – My Personal Experience

ACKNOWLEDGEMENT

This Book is dedicated to the memory of my mother, Sadie Mae (Dawkins) Craft April 20, 1936, who passed away on my birthday,
– July 16, 2016, and to my wife, Janice (Mosley) Craft, who became my better half in matrimony on February 16, 2019…YOU ARE MY LIFE!

Living with PTSD – My Personal Experience

Forward

Hello and thank-you for the purchase of my book. I thank GOD for giving me the drive and the ability to formulate the thoughts in my mind and place them into words in the form of this book about one of the most interesting, yet controversial topic today, posttraumatic stress disorder. I hope that my book adds to your reading enjoyment, knowledge, and awareness. I ask that you stay tuned for many more of my stories to come.

Living with PTSD – My Personal Experience

Introduction

Thank you for taking the time to purchase and read my book, <u>Living with PTSD - My personal experience</u>. You should want to know that this book should be made available to all individuals who are not sure but believe they are suffering from this diagnosis. The primary purpose of this book is to educate those who have experienced any traumatic event and suffer the consequences of that experience. There is a reason you get so angry on the highway when someone makes a turn and out cuts your intentions. There is a reason you often wake up in the middle of the night soaking wet from sweat and experiencing racing heartbeats. You are not alone! This book is filled with facts, information, suggestions, and lived experiences to help us to survive these circumstances until a solution has been uncovered.

Living with PTSD – My Personal Experience

For a long time in my past, as I was growing up and attending elementary school, I remember most of the people I affiliated myself with referring and relating someone being "Shell Shot," as a military veteran who had returned from combat duty and found it difficult to adjust to being home. I recall my seven childhood friends and myself sitting on a curb in the neighborhood. We were all talking about our plans to stay involved in high school sports whenever we reached that point in our lives. As we sat there talking about our dreams to someday play in the NFL or NBA, a guy was walking very slowly towards us, when one of my friends laughed aloud. The strange guy continued to walk very slowly, and he stared straight ahead until he came to where we stationed ourselves at the curb.

The strange guy pulled out a pistol and started mumbling words that we could not understand. He directed one of my friends to stand up, which he did, and he grabbed my friend from behind and said, "What you say about me!" My friend froze stiff, and he began to tell the strange guy

Living with PTSD – My Lived Experience

that he did not say anything. The strange guy placed the pistol to my friend's head and said, "You bet not be talking bout me." He soon allowed my friend to sit back down and join us on the curb, and then he walked away as slow as he approached us and continued to stare straight into space as he walked.

We later found out that the strange guy was an army veteran who was released early and medically, due to mental health concerns. I personally encountered no other situations where I noticed anyone experiencing being "shell shot." I graduated from high school in 1974 and I participated in football, cross country, and track and field. I ran track during my first year in college and was awarded Most Improved Performance in track and field while in college. Soon after track season ended during my first year of college, I decided to leave school and enter the United States Army on January 20, 1976.

One of my most treasured memories during Basic Training after entering the Army was to break the Fort Dix, New Jersey post record in the mile run. After breaking the post record in the mile, I was publicly pinned

Living with PTSD – My Lived Experience

with the "Super-jock, " badge which declared me exempt from physical exercises throughout the basic training cycle. This awards ceremony took place in a company formation as I was called to the front of the formation and was awarded the prestigious badge. IMPRESSIVE!!!!

I reported for Advanced Infantry Training (AIT) at Fort Benning, Georgia. Prior to the completion of Advanced Infantry Training, I received orders to report to my company barracks, Fort Benning, Georgia at 4:30 in the morning. The Vietnam War ended April of 1975, and my assigned company was full of soldiers who had recently returned from Vietnam. At the time I was assigned, I was the youngest soldier in the 81 mm mortar platoon.

Living with PTSD – My Personal Experience

At the age of twenty-one, as I arrived at my duty station on the first day, I noticed several pools of blood and what was later identified as brain matter on the concrete. My fellow soldiers informed that one of the soldiers committed suicide by jumping out of a third floor window. This happened again as I reported for duty another day that same week to find another pool of blood and brain matter all over the concrete. One day, as we conducted squad training on the 81 mm mortar, our attention was guided to Staff Sergeant Wilson, who dived on the ground in a prone position yelling and screaming because of a commercial airplane that he observed flying over our training site. Staff Sergeant Wilson and I became incredibly good friends after I moved into the company barracks, and he convinced me to buy and keep a liter of Seagram's Gin in my room just for him.

Living with PTSD – My Lived Experience

Every morning Staff Sergeant Wilson came to work at the barracks, he would gently tap on my barracks door at about 4:15 every morning, and say, "Let me get a shot." Staff Sergeant Wilson became my alarm clock every morning, but of course I did not mind. After taking a shot of Gin first thing in the morning, Staff Sergeant Wilson was fine for the rest of the day. Staff Sergeant Wilson advised me that the airplane flying over reminded him of an event that happened in Vietnam where a few of his comrades were killed where there was an enemy overhead flight involved.

Because I was seen by my superiors as bright, and able to matriculate math problems with ease, I was eventually trained in the Fire Direction Center (FDC) by Staff Sergeant Figueroa, who was the expert at plotting enemy targets for on a map to be targeted.

Living with PTSD – My Lived Experience

Well, my platoon leader advised me that Staff Sergeant Figueroa called his father via telephone and asked his father, "Dad, I want you to listen to this," then placed a gun to his head and committed suicide.

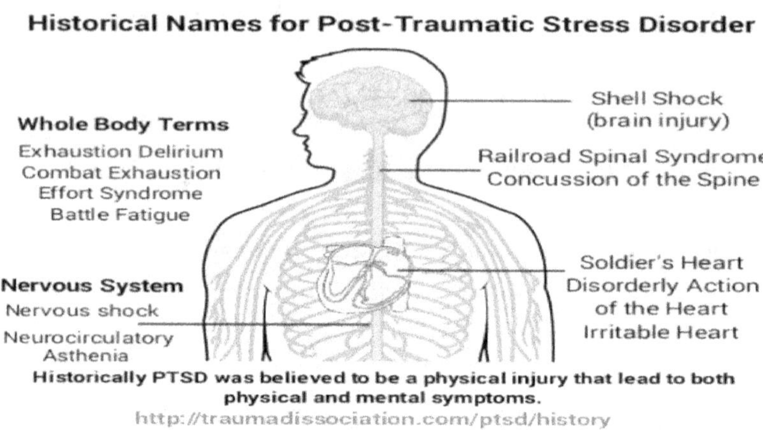

Living with PTSD – My Personal Experience

Current research concluded that between seven and twenty per cent of service members has developed some form of PTSD (as it is called today), however, a fraction of military veterans make any attempts to seek professional assistance.

Posttraumatic Stress Disorder first became the diagnosis we know today in 1980, when it was included in the Anxiety Disorders section of the DSM – III psychiatric manual. Written as followed:

DSM-III Diagnostic criteria for Post-traumatic Stress Disorder (1980)

- **A.** Existence of a recognizable stressor that would evoke significant symptoms of distress in everyone.
- **B.** Reexperiencing of the trauma as evidenced by at least one of the following:

- o (1) recurrent and intrusive recollections of the event

- o (2) recurrent dreams of the event

- o (3) sudden acting or feeling as if the traumatic event were reoccurring, because of an association with an environmental or ideational stimulus

- **C.** Numbing of responsiveness to or reduced involvement with the external world, beginning sometime after the trauma, as shown by at least one of the following:

  - o (1) markedly diminished interest in one or more significant activities

  - o (2) feeling of detachment or estrangement from others

  - o (3) constricted affect

- **D.** At least two of the following symptoms that were not present before the trauma:

Living with PTSD – My Lived Experience

- o (1) hyper alertness or exaggerated startle response

- o (2) sleep disturbance

- o (3) guilt about surviving when others have not, or about behavior required for survival

- o (4) memory impairment or trouble concentrating

- o (5) avoidance of activities that arouse recollection of the traumatic event

- o (6) intensification of symptoms by exposure to events that symbolize or resemble the traumatic event

Living with PTSD – My Lived Experience

This is the definition used today, Posttraumatic Stress Disorder (PTSD) is a psychiatric disorder that may occur in people who have experienced or witnessed a traumatic event such as a natural disaster, a serious accident, a terrorist act, war/combat, or rape or who have been threatened with death, sexual violence or severe injury. **Posttraumatic Stress Disorder does not have to be related to military, police, or and other first responder's duties.**

Living with PTSD – My Lived Experience

This is as hard for me to write today as it was to observe back in 1976, but my traumatic event involved a training incident that occurred in 1976, while attending jungle training in Panama. The 81 mm mortar platoon I was assigned to was on recon patrol during an actual live fire mission conducted by the 60 mm mortar platoon simultaneously. I served as the Radio Telephone Operator (RTO) for my platoon leader, SFC. Atkins. Part of my duties was to carry the PRC-77 Radio and to stay with the platoon leader in case he had to make any radio contacts.

The 81 mm mortar platoon distanced themselves twenty-five meters behind the first platoon as we traveled on foot through the jungle. Subsequently, one of the 60 mm mortar misfired rounds struck SFC. Cole, decapitating him from the shoulders up.

Living with PTSD – My Lived Experience

I recall all the blood and dust from the mortar round exploding, and I saw soldiers that I considered as my mentors, yelling, screaming and crying in fright. Because I was so young and inexperienced, I was truly frightened out of my mind. Everyone hit the deck (dived to the ground). I recall my platoon leader signaling to me to join him and he made a "MAY DAY" transmission over the radio to get help to us.

He advised me to come with him and we proceeded to walk towards the explosion. I saw Sergeant first class Cole lying there headless, blood everywhere when my eyes became focused on SFC Cole's right hand which was still twitching until it stopped twitching. There was one other casualty as one Private First Class was killed. I later found out that Sergeant First Class Cole was the first platoon leader, and the Private First Class was his RTO.

Living with PTSD – My Lived Experience

There was one other injury as one Sergeant received mortar round shrapnel to one of his biceps as I observed his bicep muscle blown out of his arm and hanging.

Posttraumatic Stress Disorder is characterized by symptoms of re-experiencing, avoidance, negative changes in cognitions and mood, and hyperarousal (American Psychiatric Association, 2013). PTSD symptoms may include dissociation, depression, anxiety, fear, helplessness, obsession, and social phobia and cover three sets of response-related symptoms: • Re-experiencing the traumatic event through intrusive memories, flashbacks and nightmares • Avoidance or affective numbing to traumatic experiences •
Hyperarousal/hypervigilance. Here, I highlighted the symptoms I experienced.

Living with PTSD – My Lived Experience

These symptoms adversely affect one's self-esteem, self-worth, as well as intimate and social relationships, resulting in decreased quality of life and increased suicidal ideation. With all these thoughts in my head, I always expected something very sudden and very tragic to happen. This is a reflection in my mind of how incredibly fast and unexpected my tragic event occurred.

I completed my master's degree in Rehabilitation Counseling in 2001 from South Carolina State University, while serving in law enforcement. I was hired by the South Carolina Department of Mental Health on July 16, 2012, as a Mental Health Counselor II, September of 2012. I worked at SCDMH until June 30, 2018, when I retired from the state of South Carolina.

Living with PTSD – My Lived Experience

While serving as a mental health counselor, I was providing mental health counseling to one of my clients, when she described the symptoms she was experiencing as being paranoid (peeping out of her blinds every five to ten minutes), isolation, low esteem, tired all the time due to a lack of sleep, nightmares, flashbacks, and sweating. I provided the proper services for the symptoms she described, which lead me to diagnose her PTSD.

After my client left my office, I thought about our session for a long time, and I concluded that I was experiencing some of the same symptoms as the client who just left my office. On Saturday, July 6, 2013, I walked into the VA Emergency room and explained my tragic event to the proper authorities, and the symptoms I was experiencing, and from that day until this one I have been diagnosed PTSD at 70%, and 100% overall.

Living with PTSD – My Lived Experience

I began to find myself becoming nervous when engaged with crowds of people to the point where my heart raced and skip beats from time to time. I found myself isolated and feeling better alone, peeping out of windows every five minutes or so as if expecting something tragic to occur. It never occurred to me that something was wrong, and a psychological diagnosis might result from my actions. I thought I was acting and reacting to daily situations as a normal human being. Little did I know, but my military service affected me more than I ever imagined.

I don't want you to think and believe that military experiences are the only source of traumatic events. In recent years, we have experienced mass shootings, the World Trade Center tragedy, numerous school shootings, hurricanes, tornadoes, floods and countless other catastrophes that effect our normal day mental and physical functions.

Living with PTSD – My Lived Experience

Since July 6, 2013, when I first realized that something was truly going on with me, I have been prescribed a numerous amounts of medications for depression, anxiety, insomnia and experiencing nightmares. As of today, I am being seen at Veterans Administration (VA) by psychologist, Dr. Ratchford, and have been prescribed the medications that assist with negative thoughts, sleep deprivation and nightmares/flashbacks.

The only other time I have discussed my tragic event was when I was being seen by a Veterans Administration (VA) psychologist who assigned me to write out how I felt while this tragedy was occurring. THIS WAS NOT AN EASY TASK!!!

I agreed to attend a 16-week veterans group session consisting of four veterans who met once a week and at some time during the sessions, each veteran was allowed to discuss his tragic event.

Living with PTSD – My Lived Experience

 I heard one incidence where one of the veterans in the group discussed he and other airborne soldiers being dropped into the combat zone in Vietnam and him standing next to one of his comrades one minute, turning around for a second only to find that his comrade had been shot and killed.

Another soldier made everyone aware that he cannot bare to hear "Taps" being played at any ceremony. He said if he ever hears a trumpet player whaling this song through his trumpet, his mind takes him back to Vietnam, where piles of dead bodies were burned and he recalled "Taps," being played in the background. He expressed that he experiences unbearable shaking, nervousness, shortness of breath, sweating, rapid heartbeats and startled stare.

Living with PTSD – My Lived Experience

At one point after the 16-week veterans group sessions ended, my psychologist asked me and I am sure she asked the other veterans, if the group sessions helped in any way. I honestly replied to her the group sessions were just a quick fix, because we only met once a week, but I return home every day, peeping out of the blinds and always seemingly expecting something sudden and tragic to happen. Again, I honestly told my psychologist that reliving my tragic event during the veterans group session brought back my feelings of helplessness, fear, and anxiety – the very same feeling I felt when this event occurred.

I try my best to "fit-in" when I am among crowds of people, but in the back of my mind, I'm feeling something drastic could happen at any second, or I really would prefer to be by myself right now.

Living with PTSD – My Lived Experienced

If I am driving and merging onto a highway or interstate, my mind visualizes my vehicle being struck by an 18-wheeler unexpectedly. To surmise it all, I conclude if I have an ounce of memory, I will experience total recall of my tragic event. It does not go away!

I feel more comfortable when seated facing the entrance of restaurants or public entities. This is because my mind is causing me to believe that if something tragic does happen, at least I will be able to see it transpire. Most of the time, nothing happens. There are very few times when and if I am out and about that I feel nothing tragic is going to occur.

Living with PTSD – My Lived Experience

While driving, the imagination in my mind always convey thoughts of being involved in a serious collision or something unexpected falling out of the sky or out of the trees and striking me. I often found myself waking up throughout the night, screaming, swinging, kicking, sweating, and breathing extremely hard. In my dream, I can see Sergeant First Class Cole's right hand twitching until it stopped twitching, and piles and oodles and oodles of blood.

My wife often lets me know about the uncontrollable twitching I display throughout the nights. Most times, I do not remember any of my dreams at all, so I cannot explain the twitching. It seems, I can always remember seeing Sergeant First Class Cole's body and hand twitch though.

Living with PTSD – My Lived Experience

A part of my VA treatment for PTSD involved Psychological Treatment-Based Therapies Based on feedback from veterans, because psychological therapies alone are woefully inadequate even when combined with pharmacological therapies. What I am saying here is that the veterans group sessions were supposed to help me more than just medications alone. PTSD is one of those diagnoses where a cure will never be reached but coping mechanisms can be in place to help control the symptoms. Now, do they work...well, that is another story. I can say that all medications have side effects, and I experience them all from time to time.

Here are some of the symptoms I have experience that may accompany me for the duration of my lifetime:

Living with PTSD – My Lived Experience

<u>Social interactions</u>

- Do not like people to invade my personal space

- Prefer to be alone

- Anxiety/panic attacks in public

- Difficulty sharing my feelings with others

- Prone to feelings of "road rage"

- "Stress sweat" (social situations)

- Uncomfortable in crowds

- Trouble initiating social interactions

Living with PTSD – My Lived Experience

<u>Sleep</u>

- Recurring dreams / nightmares

- Unpleasant dreams / nightmares

- Night sweats or cold sweats

- Unable to go to sleep (insomnia)

By reading this book, I want you to know, if you do not get anything else out of my writing, at least consider this – HELP IS OUT THERE SO DON'T IGNORE IT!

It is not macho to keep yourself secluded inside your living quarters, peeking out the window every five to ten minutes. It is not macho to experience waking up in the middle of the night kicking, screaming, sweating, and breathing hard, and then acting as if nothing happened.

Living with PTSD – My Lived Experience

There are counselors, psychologists, psychiatrists and therapies that can help you cope with whatever reaction to your traumatic event you experience.

Here are some important tips to remember:

- Regain confidence in yourself by identifying the problem and taking actions to deal with your concerns.

- Know and understand that reacting to a traumatic event is normal, but professional assistance is needed.

- Know and understand that you will not recover from this diagnosis overnight, it is an ongoing process.

- Know and understand that as sure as you have a memory, your traumatic event will not be forgotten, but you can learn to cope directly with your reactions.

- Know and understand that your recovery may be redirected to mean that your reactions to your event are more controllable.

- Know and understand that healing can mean that you are able to better cope with your reaction to your traumatic event.

Matthew 7:7 reads, "Ask and it shall be given to you; seek and you shall find; knock and it shall be opened to you."

I must add there is no one directory of symptoms you follow to determine a diagnosis of PTSD, because your symptoms will be dependent upon your tragic event…and how you react to it. The one thing I can say that makes me proud, was that I sought help once I realized I was experiencing PTSD symptoms. I allowed the professionals to take it from there and I agreed to every treatment that was offered on my behalf. Do not ever think, "This could never happen to me," because it most certainly can!

Living with PTSD – My Lived Experience

Remember, God Helps Those Who Help Themselves!

GOD BLESS YOU!!!

About the Author

My name is Dr. Anthony T. Craft, and I am a retired veteran Law Enforcement Officer of twenty-five years. I am also a retired Master Sergeant (E-8) from the United States Army Reserves, after serving twenty-eight years.

I earned my Ph.D. in Philosophy with a specialization in General Psychology from Northcentral University, September of 2021. I have earned two master's Degrees, the first in Rehabilitation Counseling from South Carolina State University in Orangeburg, SC., and the second in Criminal Justice from Florida Metropolitan University in Tampa, FL.

I have taught Criminal Justice classes in a college environment, which I thoroughly enjoyed. I have one daughter, Janika Shekelia Craft and two grandchildren, Devon and Daysha Grandberry. My goal is to provide helpful and exciting reading material to the public in the form of books, to assist our future investment in our children by educating them about what is happening around them every day.

Anthony presently resides in Irmo, SC.

REFERENCES

Adler A.B., Sipos M.L. (2018) Combat-Related Post-traumatic Stress Disorder: Prevalence and Risk Factors. In: Vermetten E., Germain A., Neylan T. (eds) Sleep and Combat-Related Post Traumatic Stress Disorder. Springer, New York, NY. https://doi.org/10.1007/978-1-4939-7148-0_2

American Psychiatric Association (2013). Diagnostic and statistical manual of mental diseases, fifth edition: DSM-5TM (5th ed.). Washington, DC: American Psychiatric Publishing.

Opheim, P.E., McCombs, A.B., & Waters, R.F. (2021). Scientific Basis for a Novel Combination of Cell Signaling Factors to Decrease Autonomic Over-Expression and Rebalance Dysfunctional Cell-Signaling Pathways to Attenuate Symptoms Associated with PTSD – A FOUR-Month Pre-Clinical Study – Townsend Letter, 451/452, 25-29.

Volkmar F.R. (2013) DSM-III. In: Volkmar F.R. (eds) Encyclopedia of Autism Spectrum Disorders. Springer, New York, NY. https://doi.org/10.1007/978-1-4419-1698-3_1442